Envision It! | Visual Skills Handbook

Realism and Fantasy

Literary Elements

Realism and Fantasy

Realism

Fantasy

Literary Elements

Characters

DADDY
BROTHER
SISTER
MOMMY

Setting

Plot

Beginning

Middle

End

Envision It!

Visual Strategies Handbook

Background Knowledge

Important Ideas

Inferring

Monitor and Clarify

Predict and Set Purpose

Questioning

Story Structure

Summarize

Text Structure

Visualize

Background Knowledge

Let's Think About Reading!

- What do I already know?
- What does this remind me of?

Important Ideas

Let's Think About Reading!

- What is important to know?

Inferring

Let's Think About Reading!

- What do I already know?
- How does this help me understand what happened?

Monitor and Clarify

Let's Think About Reading!

- What does not make sense?
- How can I fix it?

Predict and Set Purpose

Let's Think About Reading!

- What do I already know?
- What do I think will happen?
- What is my purpose for reading?

Questioning

Let's **Think** About **Reading!**

- What questions do I have about what I am reading?

Story Structure

Beginning

Middle

End

Let's Think About Reading!

- What happens in the beginning?
- What happens in the middle?
- What happens in the end?

Summarize

Text Structure

Let's Think About Reading!

- How is the story organized?
- Are there any patterns?

Visualize

Let's **Think** About **Reading!**

- What pictures do I see in my mind?

Program Authors

Peter Afflerbach

Camille Blachowicz

Candy Dawson Boyd

Elena Izquierdo

Connie Juel

Edward Kame'enui

Donald Leu

Jeanne R. Paratore

P. David Pearson

Sam Sebesta

Deborah Simmons

Alfred Tatum

Sharon Vaughn

Susan Watts Taffe

Karen Kring Wixson

PEARSON

Glenview, Illinois • Boston, Massachusetts • Chandler, Arizona •
Upper Saddle River, New Jersey

We dedicate Reading Street to
Peter Jovanovich.

His wisdom, courage,
and passion for education
are an inspiration to us all.

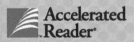

About the Cover Artist
Daniel Moreton lives in New York City, where he uses his computer to create illustrations for books. When he is not working, Daniel enjoys cooking, watching movies, and traveling. On a trip to Mexico, Daniel was inspired by all of the bright colors around him. He likes to use those colors in his art.

Acknowledgments appear on page 176, which constitute an extension of this copyright page.

ISBN-13: 978-0-328-30182-9
ISBN-10: 0-328-30182-5
10 16

CC1

Dear Reader,

A new school year is beginning. Are you ready? You are about to take a trip along a famous street—*Scott Foresman Reading Street*. On this trip you will meet a dog named Tam, a cat named Tip, and boys and girls just like you!

As you read the stories and articles, you will gain exciting new information that will help you in science and social studies.

While you're enjoying these exciting pieces of literature, you will find that something else is going on—you are becoming a better reader by gaining new skills and polishing old ones.

Have a great trip, and send us a postcard!

Sincerely,
The Authors

My World

? **What is all around me?**

Week 2

Week 3

Ready, Set, Read! Contents

Week 6

Envision It! A Comprehension Handbook

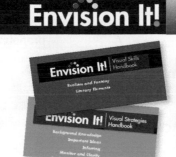

Envision It! Visual Skills Handbook EI•1–EI•6

Envision It! Visual Strategies Handbook EI•7–EI•18

Don Leu
The Internet Guy

Right before our eyes, the nature of reading and learning is changing. The Internet and other technologies create new opportunities, new solutions, and new literacies. New reading comprehension skills are required online. They are increasingly important to our students and our society.

Those of us on the Reading Street team are here to help you on this new, and very exciting, journey.

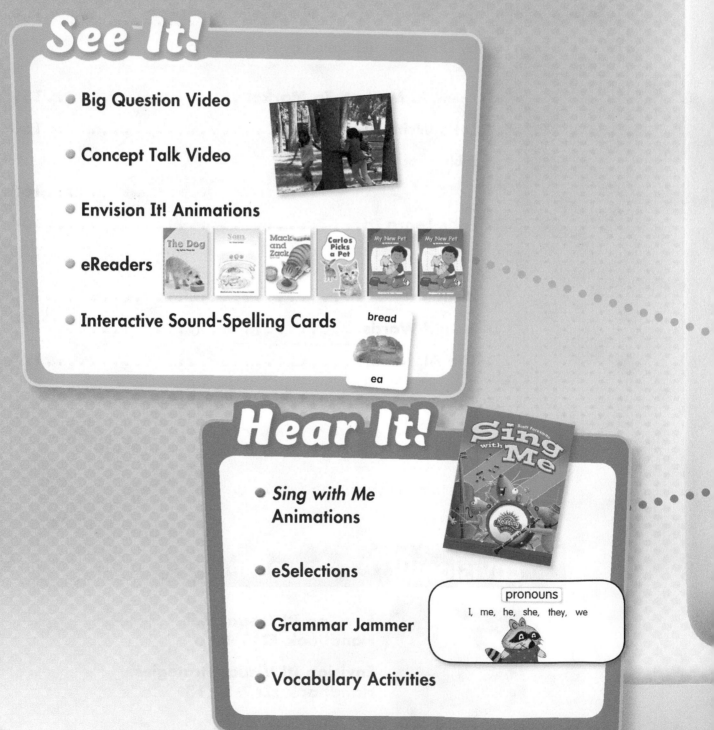

See It!

- Big Question Video

- Concept Talk Video

- Envision It! Animations

- eReaders

- Interactive Sound-Spelling Cards

Hear It!

- *Sing with Me* Animations

- eSelections

- Grammar Jammer

- Vocabulary Activities

Concept Talk Video

File   Edit   View   Favorites   Tools   Help

http://www.ReadingStreet.com

Do It!

- Journal Word Bank

- Story Sort

- Letter Tile Drag and Drop   o s c m s

- Online Assessment

- Vocabulary Activities

My World

 What is all around me?

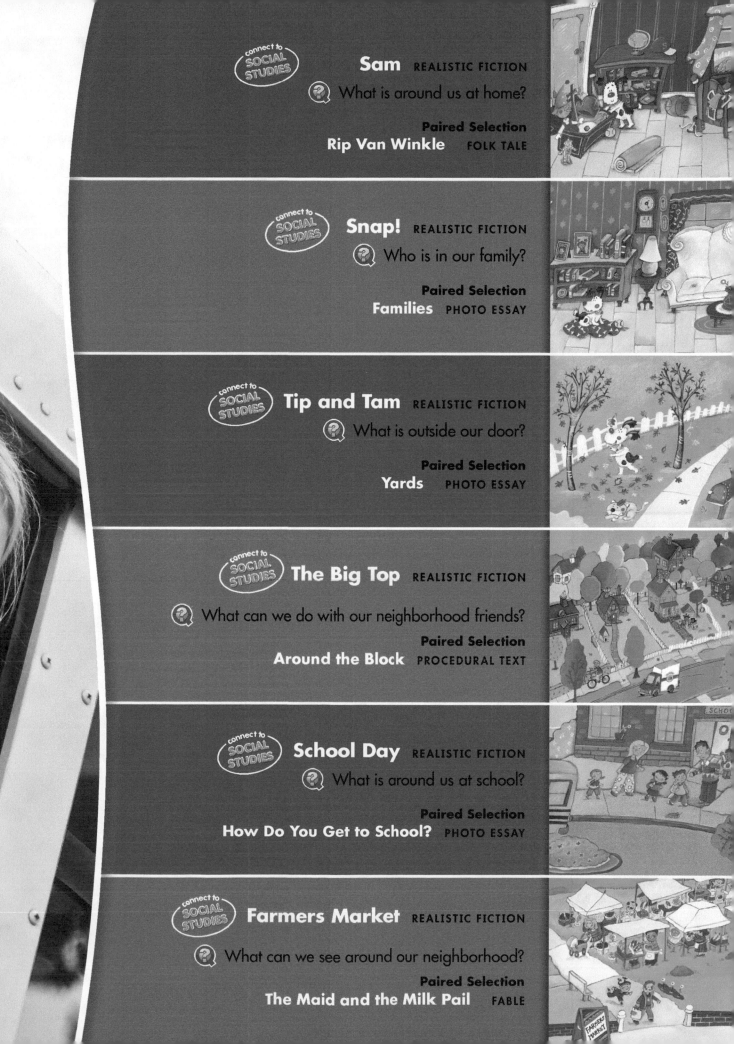

Oral Vocabulary

Let's Talk About

Read Together

Homes and Families

● Share information about life at home.

● Share ideas about what is around us at home.

READING STREET ONLINE
CONCEPT TALK VIDEO
www.ReadingStreet.com

You will learn **2 8 1** **Amazing Words** this year!

13

Phonemic Awareness

Let's Listen for

Sounds

● Find five things that begin with the sound /m/. Say the beginning sound.

● Find three things that end with the sound /s/. Say the ending sound.

● Find three things that begin with the sound /t/.

● Find something that begins with the short a sound. Say each sound in the word.

READING STREET ONLINE
SOUND-SPELLING CARDS
www.ReadingStreet.com

14

7+2   3-2
1+4   6-1
5+3

Monday
17

Envision It! | Sounds to Know

mountain

m

submarine

s

tomato

t

astronaut

short a

Phonics

Consonants *m, s, t;* Short *a*

Words I Can Blend

S	a	m
T	a	m
s	a	t
a	t	
m	a	t

Words I Can Read

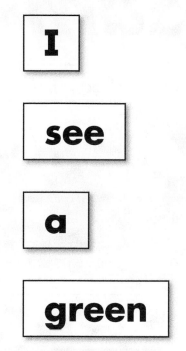

I

see

a

green

Sentences I Can Read

1. I see Sam.

2. Tam sat.

3. Sam sat at a green mat.

You've learned

⟳ Consonants *m, s, t*

⟳ Short *a*

High-Frequency Words

I   see   a   green

17

Sam

by M. C. Armstrong
illustrated by Hector Borlasca

Genre **Realistic fiction** is a kind of story. It is made-up, but it is about things that could be real.

18

Question of the Week

What is around us at home?

I am Sam. Am I Sam?

I am Tam. Am I Tam?

See Tam. Tam sat.

Sam sat. Sam sat at a mat.

Sam sat at a green mat.

Sam sat. Tam sat.

Am I Sam? Am I Tam?

Sam sat. Tam sat.

Envision It! Retell

READING STREET ONLINE
STORY SORT
www.ReadingStreet.com

Think Critically

1. What do you already know about dogs that helps you understand what Tam does? Text to Self

2. What can you learn about Sam by reading the story?

Character

3. Look Back and Write Look back at page 21. Where is Tam? Write the things you see.

TEST PRACTICE | Extended Response

Bedroom Window

Sun rises
Lights the sky
Shines through
the window's eye.

by Dee Lillegard
illustrated by Amy Cartwright

Let's Write It!

Read Together

Key Features of Nouns in Sentences

● tell about people, animals, and things

● help tell the idea of the sentence

READING STREET ONLINE
GRAMMAR JAMMER
www.ReadingStreet.com

Narrative

Nouns in Sentences

A **sentence** is a group of words that tells a complete idea. Words that name people, animals, or things are **nouns**. Most sentences have nouns.

Writing Prompt Think about a pet you would like. Write a sentence about the pet. Name the animal in your sentence.

Writer's Checklist

Remember, you should . . .

☑ write about an animal.

☑ name the animal in your sentence.

☑ begin the sentence with an uppercase, or capital, letter.

A cat can run.

I like a cat.

Each sentence starts with an uppercase, or capital, letter.

Each **sentence** tells a complete idea.

The **noun cat** names an animal.

Conventions

- ## Nouns: People, Animals, and Things

- **Remember** Some words name people, animals, or things. Naming words are called **nouns.** **Man, cup,** and **cat** are nouns. What nouns can you think of that name people, animals, or things?

hat

boy

31

Objectives
● Connect the meaning of a famous story or fable to your own experiences. ● Explain why some of the same phrases are used in different stories.

Genre
Folk Tale

Read Together

● A folk tale is a story that people have told again and again through the years. Folk tales began as oral stories, or stories that were told. Later, they were written down.

● A folk tale often begins with the phrase "Long ago." This phrase shows that the story is an old one.

● A folk tale is usually a well-known story. Sometimes the meaning of a folk tale can be connected to a reader's personal experiences.

● Read "Rip Van Winkle." Think about what makes it a folk tale.

Rip Van Winkle

Long ago, Rip Van Winkle climbed up a hill. He fell asleep.

Rip slept for many years! He told his story again and again. People liked to hear the story.

Let's **Think** About...

This story begins with the phrase "Long ago." What does that tell you? **Folk Tale**

Let's **Think** About...

How can you connect what happened to Rip to something that has happened to you? **Folk Tale**

Let's **Think** About...

Reading Across Texts Tell what Sam does in *Sam*. Tell what Rip does in "Rip Van Winkle." Which actions could really happen?

Writing Across Texts Imagine Rip tells his story to Sam. What does Sam think of the story? Write about what Sam thinks.

Objectives
- Understand and use words that name actions, called *verbs*. Understand and use words that name people, places, or things, called *nouns*.
- Identify and put words into groups based on what they mean. • Understand and use nouns when reading, writing, and speaking. • Listen closely to speakers and ask questions to help you better understand the topic.
- Follow rules for discussions such as listening to others, speaking when your teacher calls on you, and making comments about the topic.

Let's take turns talking. Then we will be able to hear what each of us says.

Let's Learn It!

Read Together

**READING STREET ONLINE
VOCABULARY ACTIVITIES**
www.ReadingStreet.com

Listening and Speaking

Get Ready For Grade 2

Follow agreed-upon rules in a group discussion.

Participate in a Discussion When we work in a group, we follow rules of discussion. We listen to each other and talk when someone calls our name. We stay on topic.

Practice It! Think about the story you read this week—*Sam.* Follow the rules. Listen to others. Take turns telling about something you liked in the story. Use nouns as you speak.

Vocabulary

A **noun** is a word that names a person, an animal, a place, or a thing. We can sort nouns into groups.

bear

horse

monkey

These nouns are all names for animals.

Practice It! Read these words. Sort them into categories of people, animals, places, or things.

boy   bus   girl   home   tree

Handwriting

Proper Body Position Be sure to sit up straight when you write. Write neatly, from left to right and from top to bottom. Look at the models on pages 174–175. Then write a row of these letters:

Mm   Tt   Ss   Aa

Oral Vocabulary

Let's Talk About

Read Together

Homes and Families

● Share information about families.

● Share ideas about who is in our families.

Objectives
● Say a group of words that rhyme using different groups of letters.
● Pick out sounds at the beginning, in the middle, and at the end of one-syllable words. ● Combine sounds together to say words with one and two syllables.

Let's Listen for

Sounds

Read Together

● Find five things that begin with the sound /p/. Say the beginning sound.

● Find two things that rhyme with *fan*. Say the ending sound.

● Find five things that begin with the sound /n/.

● Find something that rhymes with *map*. Say each sound in the word.

READING STREET ONLINE
SOUND-SPELLING CARDS
www.ReadingStreet.com

ZOO

9

38

Objectives
● Decode words with consonants.
● Identify and read at least 100 words from a list of words that you use often.

Envision It! | Sounds to Know

carrot

c

pilot

p

READING STREET ONLINE
SOUND-SPELLING CARDS
www.ReadingStreet.com

Phonics

🎯 Consonants *c, p*

Words I Can Blend

c	a	p
c	a	t
p	a	t
t	a	p
m	a	p

Words I Can Read

we

like

one

the

Sentences I Can Read

1. We pat one cat.

2. I like a cap.

3. Sam, tap the map.

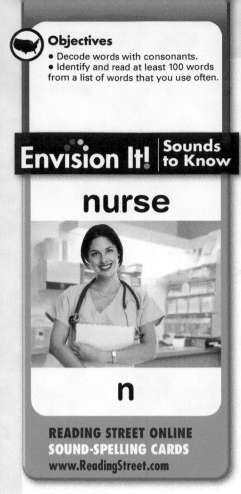

Envision It! | Sounds to Know

nurse

n

READING STREET ONLINE
SOUND-SPELLING CARDS
www.ReadingStreet.com

Phonics

Consonant *n*

Words I Can Blend

c a n

m a n

p a n

n a p

t a n

42

One tan cat sat. Sam can pat the tan cat. Matt can pat the tan cat.

We like Sam. We like Matt. We like the tan cat. The tan cat can nap.

Nap, tan cat! Nap!

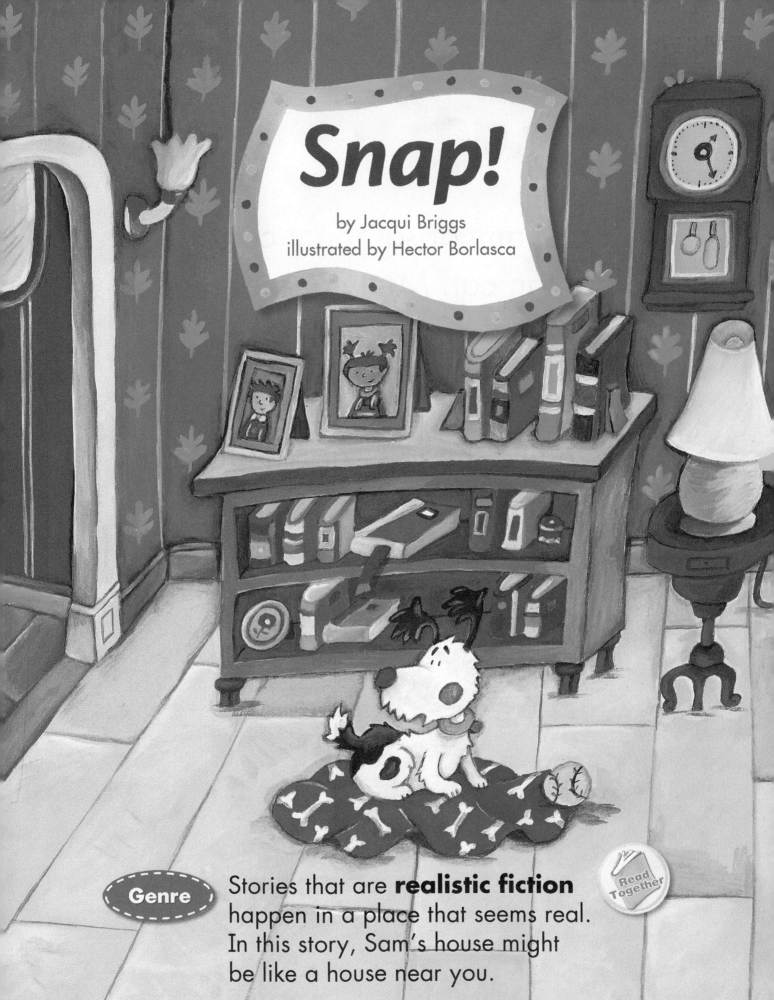

Snap!

by Jacqui Briggs
illustrated by Hector Borlasca

Genre Stories that are **realistic fiction** happen in a place that seems real. In this story, Sam's house might be like a house near you.

Read Together

44

Question of the Week

Who is in our family?

I am Sam.

I can tap one pan.

Pam can tap at the tan mat.

Tap, Pam, tap!

Tap, tap, tap! We can tap!

Tam sat. I can pat Tam.

Pat, pat, pat!

Pam can pat Tam.

Pat, pat, pat!

I see Mac. We like Mac.

Mac can snap.

Mac can snap.

Snap, snap, snap!

Snap Pam. Snap Sam.

Tam can nap. Snap, snap!

Envision It! Retell

Think Critically

Read Together

1. What does Mac do? Where else might someone like Mac work? **Text to World**

2. Where does this story happen? **Setting**

3. **Look Back and Write** Look back at pages 51 and 52. Who comes to Sam's house? Write about what this person does.

TEST PRACTICE Extended Response

My Family

Part of my family is
grown-up and tall.

Part of my family is
little and small.

I'm in the middle
and pleased with them all.

by Marchette Chute
illustrated by Wednesday Kirwan

Let's Write It!

Read Together

Key Features of Nouns in Sentences

● can tell about places

● help tell the idea of the sentence

READING STREET ONLINE
GRAMMAR JAMMER
www.ReadingStreet.com

Nouns in Sentences

A **sentence** is a group of words that tells a complete idea. A noun in a sentence can name a place, such as a *store*, *park*, or *house*.

Writing Prompt Think about a place you go during the day. Write about the place. Tell the name of the place in your sentence.

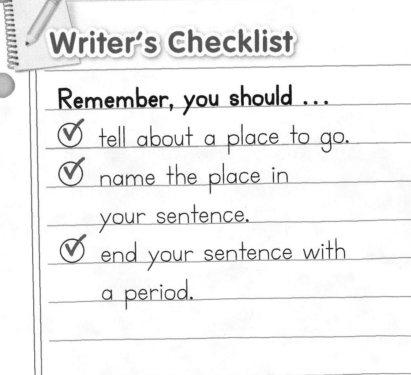

Writer's Checklist

Remember, you should . . .

☑ tell about a place to go.

☑ name the place in your sentence.

☑ end your sentence with a period.

My mom and I walk to the store.

The sentence tells a complete idea.

The **noun store** names a place.

A **period** ends the sentence.

Conventions

- ## Nouns: Places

- **Remember** Some nouns name places. **Room, store,** and **park** are all nouns that name places. What other nouns can you think of that name places?

farm

school

57

Social Studies in Reading

Genre
Photo Essay

Read Together

- The word *photo* is a short way to say *photograph*.

- A photo essay is made up of photographs and words. The photographs help explain the words.

- All the photographs and words in a photo essay are about the same topic.

- Read "Families." As you read, look for elements of a photo essay. Ask yourself questions about the text.

Families

A family is a group of people who love each other.

Families play together.
Families eat together.

Families read together.
What does your family
like to do together?

Let's **Think** About...

What do these photographs show about the topic of families? What questions do you have?
Photo Essay

Let's **Think** About...

Reading Across Texts How are photographs important in both *Snap!* and "Families"?

Writing Across Texts Draw pictures of a family from each selection doing something together. Write a sentence that tells about each picture.

59

Objectives
● Understand and use nouns when reading, writing, and speaking.
● Understand and use adjectives when reading, writing, and speaking. ● Share information and ideas about the topic. Speak at the correct pace. ● Print upper- and lower-case letters clearly from left-to-write and top-to-bottom, and leave enough space between words and between sentences.

Cass and I had our picture taken. Mac took the picture.

Read Together

Let's **Learn** It!

READING STREET ONLINE
VOCABULARY ACTIVITIES
www.ReadingStreet.com

Listening and Speaking

Get Ready For Grade 2

Share ideas by telling about something that happened.

Share Ideas When we tell others about things that we do, we make sure to speak clearly. We tell about what happened and how it happened.

Practice It! Think of something that happened to you. Tell others about it. Speak clearly and slowly. Use a noun for each person, place, or thing that you mention.

Vocabulary

A descriptive word, or **adjective,** is a word that tells about people, places, animals, or things.

tall

green

Green and *tall* are words that describe the tree.

Practice It! Think about an apple. Choose words that might describe it.

green   red   shiny   funny

Handwriting

Proper Letter Size When you write, it should be easy to tell the difference between letters that are tall, letters that are small, and letters that fall. Write neatly, from left to right and from top to bottom. Look at the models on pages 174–175. Then write a row of these letters: **Cc   Pp   Nn**

Let's Talk About

Read Together

About

Homes and Families

● Share information about life outside at home.

● Share ideas about what is outside our door.

READING STREET ONLINE
CONCEPT TALK VIDEO
www.ReadingStreet.com

Let's Listen for

Sounds

● Find five things that begin with the sound /f/. Say the sound.

● Find five things that begin with the sound /b/. Say the sound.

● Find three things that end with the sound /g/. Say the sound.

● Find something that rhymes with *wall*. Say each sound in the word.

● Find three things that contain the short *i* sound.

READING STREET ONLINE
SOUND-SPELLING CARDS
www.ReadingStreet.com

Read Together

Objectives
● Decode words with consonants.
● Identify and read at least 100 words from a list of words that you use often.

Envision It! | **Sounds to Know**

firefighter

f

butterfly

b

READING STREET ONLINE
SOUND-SPELLING CARDS
www.ReadingStreet.com

Consonants *f, b*

Words I Can Blend

f	a	n
f	a	t
b	a	t
n	a	b
c	a	b

Words I Can Read

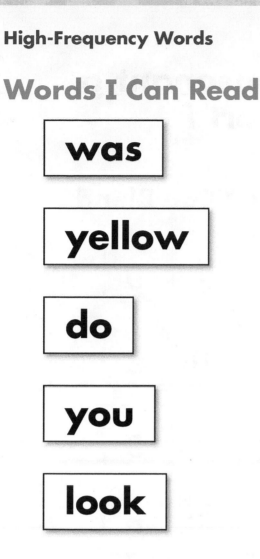

was

yellow

do

you

look

Sentences I Can Read

1. One fan was yellow.

2. Do you see the fat bat?

3. Look at Cass nab a cab.

Objectives
• Decode words with consonants.
• Identify and read at least 100 words from a list of words that you use often.

Envision It! | Sounds to Know

game

g

insects

short i

READING STREET ONLINE
SOUND-SPELLING CARDS
www.ReadingStreet.com

Phonics

Consonant *g*, Short *i*

Words I Can Blend

b i g

b a g

p i g

p i n

i t

I Can Read!

A yellow pig sat in a big bin.

Look at it, Tim. Do you see it?
A pig can sit in the big bin. A
fat cat can sit in the big bin.

It was a big, big bin.

You've learned

- Consonants f, b, g
- Short i

High-Frequency Words
was   yellow   do   you   look

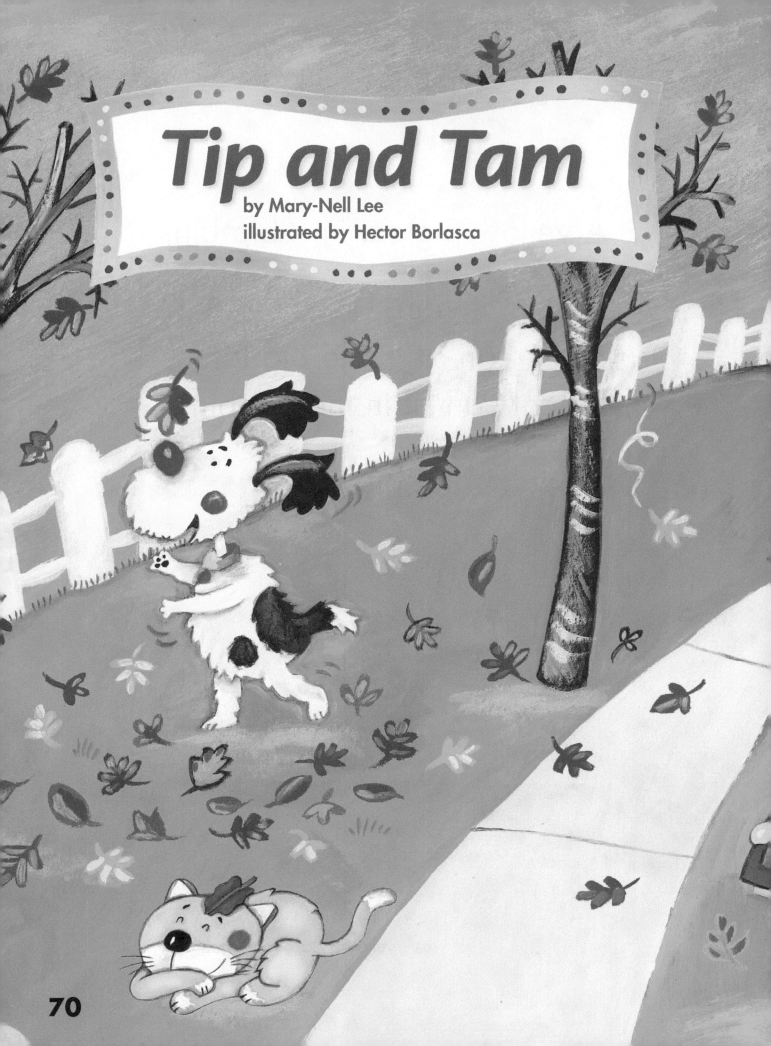

Tip and Tam

by Mary-Nell Lee

illustrated by Hector Borlasca

Realistic fiction tells about things that could really happen, but the stories are made up. Next you will read about friends who are made-up characters.

Question of the Week

What is outside our door?

Nan can tap Sam.

Pat can tap Pam.

Sam can tap Pat.

Pam can tap Nan.

Do you see Tip?

Look at the yellow cat.

Tip can bat the big tan bag.

Tam can nip at it.

Tam can sit in the big bag!

Tip can fit in it.

Can Pam see Tip?

Can Sam see Tam?

Look at the fat tan bag!

Tip was in the big tan bag!

Tam sat in it!

Envision It! | Retell

Think Critically

1. What are Sam and his friends doing in the yard? What have you seen people doing in their yards? Text to Self

2. What happens at the end of the story? Why is it important? Plot

3. **Look Back and Write**
Look back at page 79. Where are Tip and Tam? Write about how you know.

TEST PRACTICE | Extended Response

Home

All around me quiet.

All around me peaceful.

All around me lasting.

All around me home.

Ute Indian poem
illustrated by Susan Mitchell

Read
Together

Let's Write It!

Key Features of Verbs in Sentences

● tell about what we do

● help tell the idea of the sentence

READING STREET ONLINE
GRAMMAR JAMMER
www.ReadingStreet.com

Verbs in Sentences

A **sentence** tells a complete idea. Some words in sentences tell what we do. Words that tell actions are **verbs**. All sentences have verbs.

Writing Prompt Think about something you do with friends. Write about what you and your friends do. Use a verb in your sentence.

Writer's Checklist

Remember, you should . . .

☑ write about something you do with friends.

☑ use a verb in your sentence.

☑ begin the sentence with an uppercase, or capital, letter.

We play games.

This sentence begins with an uppercase, or capital, *W*.

The **sentence** tells what the writer and other children do.

The **verb play** tells about an action.

Conventions

jump

skip

Verbs

Remember Some words are action words. Action words are called **verbs**. Verbs tell what we do. **Run, talk,** and **play** are verbs. What verbs can you say?

Genre
Photo Essay

Read Together

- In a photo essay, photographs and words work together to tell about one topic.

- A photo essay may inform or entertain readers.

- Photo essays show real people, places, and events. They can be photographs from the past or from the present.

- As you read "Yards," think about what makes it a photo essay.

Yards

A yard is a piece of ground near a house or building.

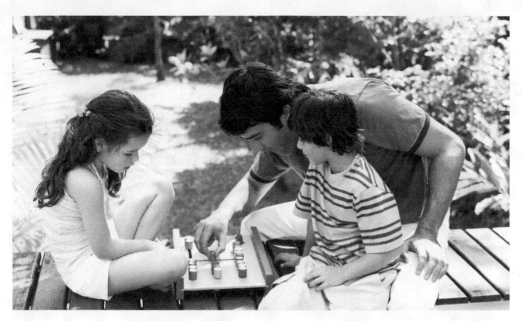

Yards can be in the front or the back. A yard can be a nice place to play or relax.

Let's **Think** About...

How do these photos help readers understand what a yard is?
Photo Essay

Have you ever seen a yard like this?

Let's **Think** About...

Reading Across Texts Which yard shown in the photo essay "Yards" is most like the yard in the story *Tip and Tam*? How?

Writing Across Texts Draw pictures of things you might see in a yard. Use the selections to help you.

First I'll write my name on my paper. Then, I'll write a sentence. I will circle the period at the end of my sentence.

Let's Learn It!

Read Together

Listening and Speaking

Get Ready For Grade 2

Restate instructions before you follow them.

Follow, Restate, Give Instructions We listen carefully to instructions we're given. Then we say them again, or restate them, to make sure we remember what we're supposed to do.

Practice It! Have a partner give you instructions. Restate the instructions, and then follow them. Say the verbs that tell what you do. Then you give instructions to your partner. Your partner should restate the directions and then follow them.

Vocabulary

A **noun** names a person, animal, place, or thing. A **verb** is a word that tells an action. We can sort nouns and verbs.

ball

Ball is a noun.

Climb is a verb.

climb

Practice It! Read the words. Identify and sort the nouns and verbs.

bed   **hide**   **man**   **swim**

Handwriting

Proper Paper Position Be sure your paper is slanted correctly on your desk when you write. Write neatly, from left to right and from top to bottom. Look at the models on pages 174–175. Then write a row of these letters:

Ff   **Bb**   **Gg**   **Ii**

Objectives
• Listen closely to speakers and ask questions to help you better understand the topic. • Share information and ideas about the topic. Speak at the correct pace.

Let's Talk About

Read Together

Neighborhoods

- Share information about neighborhoods.

- Share ideas about what we can do with our neighborhood friends.

READING STREET ONLINE
CONCEPT TALK VIDEO
www.ReadingStreet.com

You've learned

0 2 2

Amazing Words

so far this year!

89

Objectives
• Say a group of words that rhyme using different groups of letters. • Pick out sounds at the beginning, in the middle, and at the end of one-syllable words. • Combine sounds together to say words with one and two syllables.

Let's Listen for

Sounds

Read Together

● Find five things that begin with the sound /d/. Say the sound.

● Find two things that end with the sound /l/. Say the sound.

● Find three things that begin with the sound /h/.

● Find three things that rhyme with *hop*. Say each sound in the word.

READING STREET ONLINE
SOUND-SPELLING CARDS
www.ReadingStreet.com

Play Village

grocer

CITY HALL

90

Play Village

Objectives
- Decode words with consonants.
- Identify and read at least 100 words from a list of words that you use often.

Envision It! | Sounds to Know

dime

d

ladder

l

Phonics

🎯 Consonants *d, l*

Words I Can Blend

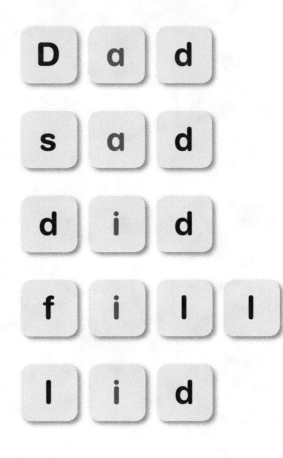

D	a	d
s	a	d
d	i	d
f	i	l	l
l	i	d

Words I Can Read

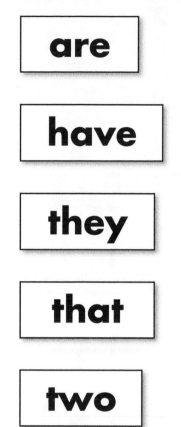

are

have

they

that

two

Sentences I Can Read

1. Are they in a can, Dad?

2. We have a sad cat.

3. Two did fill that big lid!

Phonics

Consonant *h*, Short *o*

Words I Can Blend

h o p

d o l l

h o t

g o t

h a t

I have a big doll. Doll can hop.
Hop, Doll, hop! Doll can hop
on a hill.

Two can look at Doll hop.

It got hot on that hill. The two
got a hat. They are not hot.

You've learned

- Consonants *d, l, h*
- Short *o*

High-Frequency Words
are   have   they   that   two

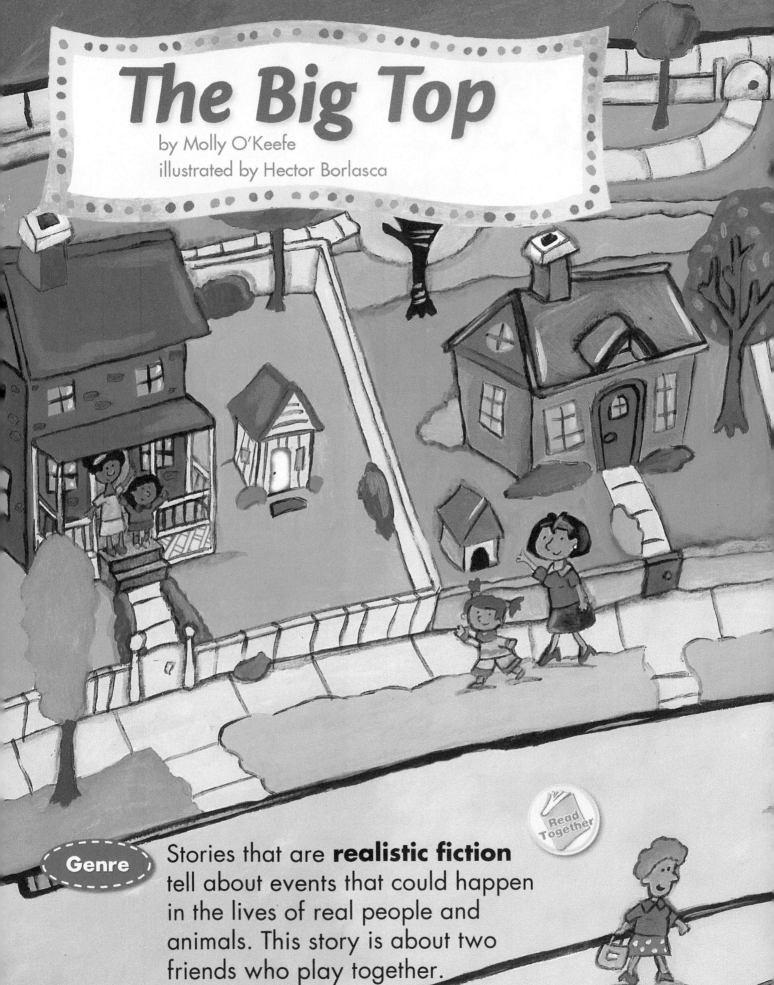

The Big Top

by Molly O'Keefe

illustrated by Hector Borlasca

Genre

Stories that are **realistic fiction** tell about events that could happen in the lives of real people and animals. This story is about two friends who play together.

Question of the Week

What can we do with our neighborhood friends?

97

Pam and Dot can hop and hop.

One, two. They can hop fast.

Dot and Pam sat.

Dot and Pam are on the mat.

A doll sat on the mat.

Tip hit the doll. Stop, Tip, stop!

A big top sat on the mat.

Tip can see it.

Dot got the big top.

Tip did not like that top!

Tip hid.

Dot and Pam sat.

Tip hit the big top.

Tip bit it. Stop, Tip, stop!

Pam and Dot stop Tip.

Pam and Dot have the big top.

Objectives
• Describe the problem and the solution of a story. Retell a story's beginning, middle, and end in the order in which the events happened. • Read on your own for a period of time.

Envision It! | Retell

Think Critically

1. Tip did not like the big top. Tell what you would do to help. Text to Self

2. Could this story really happen? Explain.

Realism and Fantasy

3. Look Back and Write Look back at pages 98 and 99. What do Pam and Dot like to do? Write about it.

TEST PRACTICE Extended Response

READING STREET ONLINE
STORY SORT
www.ReadingStreet.com

106

Meet the Illustrator

Hector Borlasca

Hector Borlasca loves to illustrate books because it brings a new surprise every day. He hopes that children see something new every time they look at his illustrations.

Here is another book illustrated by Hector Borlasca.

AGUSTINA
se duerme

Reading Log

Use the Reading Log in the *Reader's and Writer's Notebook* to record your independent reading.

107

Let's Write It!

Read Together

Key Features of a Simple Sentence

- tells a complete idea
- begins with an uppercase letter
- can end with a period

READING STREET ONLINE
GRAMMAR JAMMER
www.ReadingStreet.com

Simple Sentences

A **sentence** tells a complete idea. A sentence begins with an uppercase letter. Most sentences end with a period.

Writing Prompt Think about something a cat can do. Write a sentence about a cat. Tell what it does.

Writer's Checklist

Remember, you should . . .

☑ write about something a cat does.

☑ begin your sentence with an uppercase letter.

☑ end your sentence with a period. Say your sentence.

The cat runs to the mat.

An uppercase, or capital, **T** begins the sentence.

This **sentence** tells what a cat does.

A **period** ends the sentence.

Conventions

- **Simple Sentences**

  Remember A sentence is
- a group of words that tells a complete idea. It begins with an uppercase letter. Many
- sentences end with a **period.**

  Say this sentence.
- **Pam sat.**

  This is not a sentence.
  Pam and Dot

109

Social Studies in Reading

Genre
Procedural Text

Read Together

● Some selections use words along with signs and symbols.

● A sign tells you what to do.

● A symbol is a picture that stands for something else.

● Read "Around the Block." As you read, remember what you learned about signs and symbols.

Around the Block

There are many signs and symbols in our neighborhood.

110

Signs and symbols
help us drive.

Signs and symbols
help us ride.

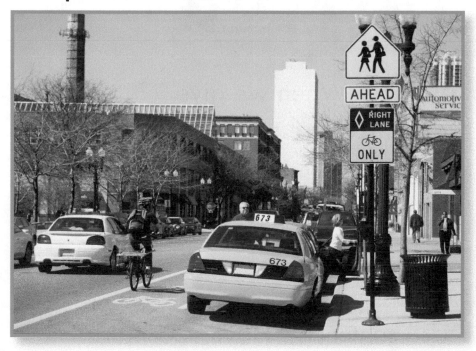

Signs and symbols help
keep us safe.

Let's **Think** About...

What signs and symbols do you see on these pages?
Procedural Text

Let's **Think** About...

What do the signs and symbols tell you?
Procedural Text

Let's **Think** About...

Reading Across Texts What kinds of street signs might Pam see in her neighborhood?

Writing Across Texts Draw a picture of some signs and symbols Pam might see in her neighborhood. Write a label for each.

First, open your book to page 24. Then, read the page. Last, close your book and put it in your desk.

Let's Learn It!

Read Together

**READING STREET ONLINE
VOCABULARY ACTIVITIES**
www.ReadingStreet.com

Get Ready For Grade 2

Speak clearly when you give instructions.

Listening and Speaking

Give Instructions When we give instructions, we make sure to speak clearly. We make sure our instructions are easy to follow.

Practice It! Give a partner some simple instructions. Use sentences. Have your partner restate the instructions and follow them.

Vocabulary

Words that tell about or describe something are descriptive words, or **adjectives.** We can identify and sort adjectives that describe the way something looks, tastes, smells, feels, or sounds.

sweet grapes

The word *sweet* describes how the grapes taste.

Practice It! Read these words. Write and say the words that tell how something feels.

rough   **loud**   **smooth**   **spicy**

Handwriting

Proper Letter Size When you write, your letters should fit properly on the lines of your paper. Look at the models on pages 174–175. Then write a row of these letters:

Dd   **Ll**   **Hh**   **Oo**

Use the models to write these words, being sure to leave space between the words:

doll   **old**   **hood**

Let's Talk About

Read Together

Neighborhoods

● Share information about what is around us at school.

● Share ideas about what we do at school each day.

READING STREET ONLINE
CONCEPT TALK VIDEO
www.ReadingStreet.com

114

You've learned
0 3 0
Amazing Words
so far this year!

Objectives
- Say a group of words that rhyme using different groups of letters.
- Combine sounds together to say words with one and two syllables.
- Pick out sounds at the beginning, in the middle, and at the end of one-syllable words.

Let's Listen for

Sounds

- Find four things that begin with the sound /r/. Say the sound.

- Find three things that begin with the sound /w/. Say the sound.

- Find two things that begin with the sound /j/.

- Find two things that begin with the sound /k/.

- Find something that rhymes with *wet*. Say each sound in the word.

Read Together

READING STREET ONLINE
SOUND-SPELLING CARDS
www.ReadingStreet.com

116

Objectives
• Decode words with consonants.
• Decode words by using letter-sound patterns to understand the different sounds vowels make. • Identify and read at least 100 words from a list of words that you use often.

Envision It! | Sounds to Know

rocket

r

waterfall

w

jacket

j

READING STREET ONLINE
SOUND-SPELLING CARDS
www.ReadingStreet.com

Phonics

Consonants *r, w, j*

Words I Can Blend

j a m

r a n

w i n

w i l l

r i m

Words I Can Read

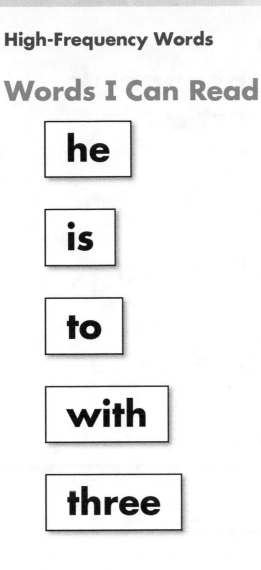

he

is

to

with

three

Sentences I Can Read

1. He is in a jam.

2. Three ran to win.

3. Jim will sit on the rim with Jill.

Objectives
- Decode words with consonants.
- Decode words by using letter-sound patterns to understand the different sounds vowels make. • Identify and read at least 100 words from a list of words that you use often.

Envision It! **Sounds to Know**

kite

k

elephant

short e

**READING STREET ONLINE
SOUND-SPELLING CARDS**
www.ReadingStreet.com

Phonics

🎯 Consonant *k*, Short *e*

Words I Can Blend

| k | i | d |

| g | e | t |

| k | i | s | s |

| w | e | t |

| t | e | l | l |

Ken is three. He is a kid I met on a jet. Ken had a red bell with him.

Is a bell on a jet bad? Men on the jet tell Ken to sell that red bell. Will Ken get in a jam?

You've learned

- Consonants *r, w, j, k*
- Short *e*

High-Frequency Words

he   is   to   with   three

School Day

by Cass Stricker

illustrated by Hector Borlasca

Genre In **realistic fiction,** the people and events are made-up. Sam and his friends are made-up characters who do real things, like go to school.

SCHOOL

Question of the Week

What is around us at school?

123

Sam is still in bed!

Mom will get him.

Grab the red bag, Sam!

Sam ran fast. He got on.

Sam sat with Fred.

Sam met Pat, Kim, and Jill.

The three tell the plan to Sam.

Pat did a jet kit. Jill will jig.

Kim will sit on a mat.

The red bag had a rip!

Fred will drop! Stop him!

Sam is sad. Kim will help him.

Jill and Pat will help him.

They will help Fred.

Sam is not sad.

Envision It! | Retell

Think Critically

1. How is Sam's school like your school? Text to Self

2. What happens in the beginning of the story? What happens at the end?

   Plot

3. **Look Back and Write**
   Look back at page 128. What will Kim, Jill, and Pat do?

   TEST PRACTICE Extended Response

School Bus

Friendly fellow
Dressed in yellow
Greets his kids
With a beep-beep hello!

by Dee Lillegard
illustrated by Dean MacAdam

Let's Write It!

Read Together

Key Features of Sentences with Adjectives

● tell complete ideas

● describe people, places, animals, or things

READING STREET ONLINE
GRAMMAR JAMMER
www.ReadingStreet.com

Expressive

Sentences with Adjectives

A **sentence** tells a complete idea. Words that describe people, places, animals, or things are **adjectives.** A sentence may have an adjective or more than one adjective.

Writing Prompt Think about your favorite things. Write a sentence about one of them. Use an adjective to tell about the thing.

Writer's Checklist

Remember, you should . . .

☑ write a sentence about a thing that you like.

☑ use an adjective to describe the thing.

☑ end the sentence with a period.

I like my blue hat.

The sentence tells a complete idea.

The **adjective blue** tells about the hat.

A period ends the **sentence.**

Conventions

- **Adjectives**

  Some words tell more about people, places, animals, or things. Describing words are called **adjectives. Green, big, tall,** and **little** are adjectives. What other adjectives can you say?

happy

red

135

Genre
Photo Essay

Read Together

- The words and photographs in a photo essay are about the same topic. The words tell and the photographs show.

- The photographs in a photo essay are usually memorable. The photographer wants you to feel as if you were there.

- Photographs help readers connect with real people, places, and events, even from different parts of the world.

- Read "How Do You Get to School?" Think about what you learned about photo essays.

How Do You Get to School?

Children go to school every day.
There are many ways to get to school.

Jelani walks to school.
Aisha rides a rickshaw.
How do you get to
school?

Let's **Think** About...

How do you think the person who took these photographs wants you to feel?
Photo Essay

Let's **Think** About...

Reading Across Texts How does Sam in *School Day* get to school? How do the children shown in the photo essay get to school?

Writing Across Texts Draw pictures of the ways Sam and the children get to school. Label the pictures.

Read Together

Let's Learn It!

READING STREET ONLINE
VOCABULARY ACTIVITIES
www.ReadingStreet.com

I ride a bus to go to school. Sometimes my dad drops me off instead.

When your dad drops you off, do you ride in a car?

Get Ready For Grade 2

Ask questions if you don't understand a speaker.

Listening and Speaking

Ask Questions If we're confused about something a speaker says, we ask him or her to explain.

 Have a partner tell you something. Listen carefully. Ask questions if you don't understand. Then tell something to your partner. When your partner asks you questions, listen carefully to each one so that you know exactly what your partner is asking. Then answer the questions.

138

Vocabulary

A descriptive word, or **adjective,** tells about people, animals, places, or things.

little

The word *little* describes the bird.

The little bird flies.

Practice It! Read these words. Write and say a descriptive word for each one.

bus   **cat**   **friend**   **bike**

Handwriting

Proper Body Position Keep both feet flat on the floor when you write. Look at the models on pages 174–175. Then write a row of these letters:

Rr   Ww   Jj   Kk   Ee

Use the models to write these words, being sure to leave space between the words:

week   jar   Kirk

Let's Talk About

Neighborhoods

- Share information about what we see around our neighborhood.

- Share ideas about places we can go and things we can do in our neighborhood.

READING STREET ONLINE
CONCEPT TALK VIDEO
www.ReadingStreet.com

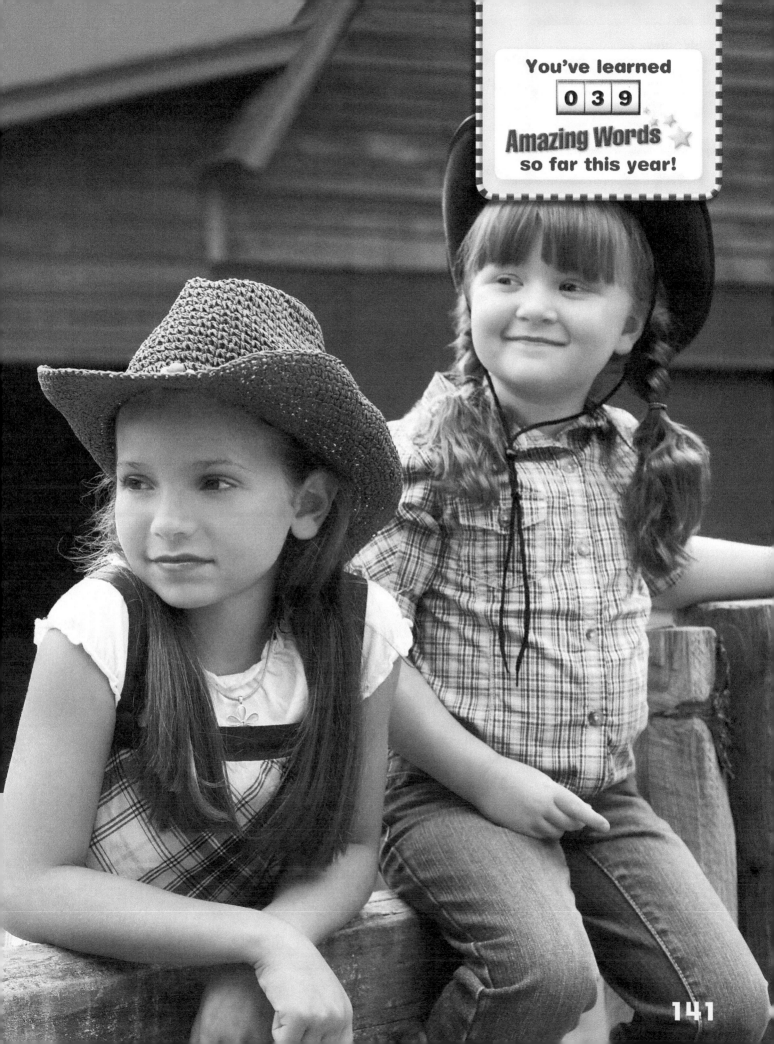

Objectives

- Combine sounds together to say words with one and two syllables.
- Pick out sounds at the beginning, in the middle, and at the end of one-syllable words.
- Break up one-syllable words into each sound that makes up the word.

Let's Listen for

Sounds

- Find five things that begin with the sound /v/. Say the beginning sound.

- Find two things that begin with the sound /y/.

- Find three things that begin with the sound /z/.

- Find two things that rhyme with *hum*.

- Find two things that begin with the sound /kw/. Say each sound in one of those words.

READING STREET ONLINE
SOUND-SPELLING CARDS
www.ReadingStreet.com

142

Objectives
• Decode words with consonants.
• Decode words by using letter-sound patterns to understand the different sounds vowels make. • Identify and read at least 100 words from a list of words that you use often.

Envision It! | Sounds to Know

volcano

v

yo-yo

y

zebra

z

Phonics

Consonants v, y, z

Words I Can Blend

y a m

v a n

y e s

z i p

j a z z

Words I Can Read

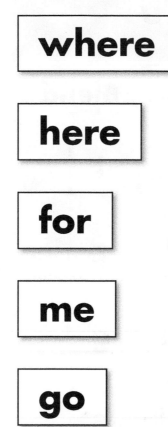

Sentences I Can Read

1. Yaz will get me the yam in the van.

2. Mom can zip it here.

3. Where can Val go for jazz?

Envision It! | Sounds to Know

quilt

qu

umbrella

short u

Phonics

Consonant *qu*, Short *u*

Words I Can Blend

qu	i	t
qu	i	z
h	u	g
b	u	s
s	u	n

Here is a quiz for us. Where can we go on a bus? A bus can get us to a vet. It can zip us to fun in the sun.

Yes, a bus will not quit. Get on a bus with me!

You've learned

⊙ Consonants *v, y, z, qu*

⊙ Short *u*

High-Frequency Words
where   here   for   me   go

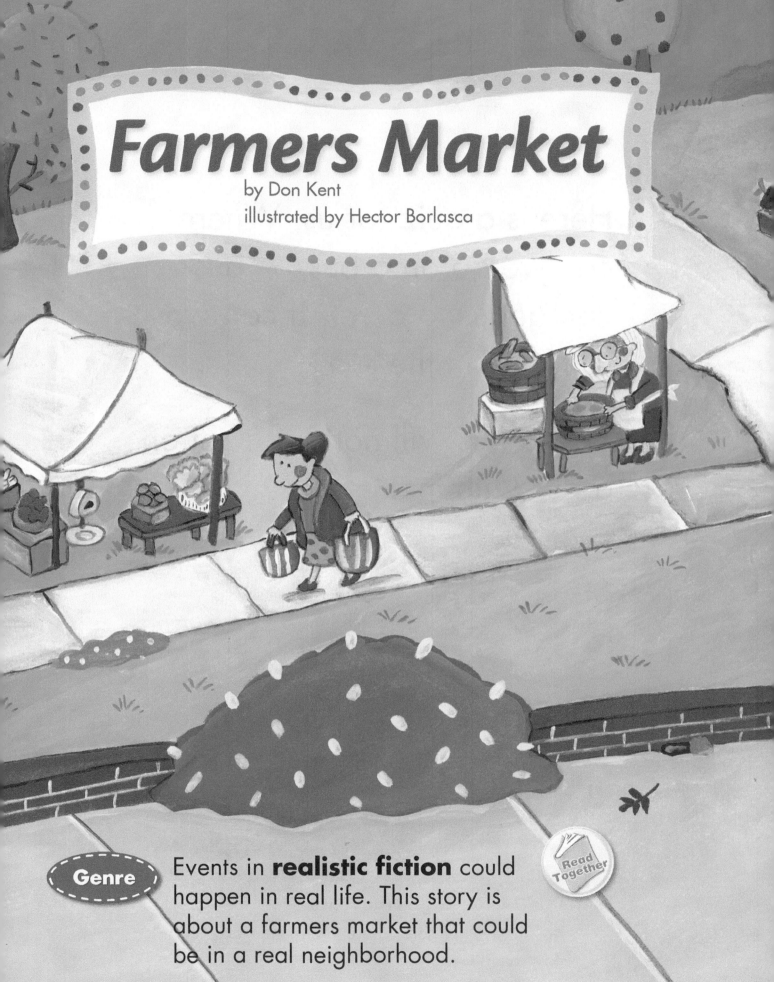

Farmers Market

by Don Kent

illustrated by Hector Borlasca

Genre Events in **realistic fiction** could happen in real life. This story is about a farmers market that could be in a real neighborhood.

Read Together

148

What can we see around our neighborhood?

149

Pam and Dad get on the bus.

Where will the bus go?

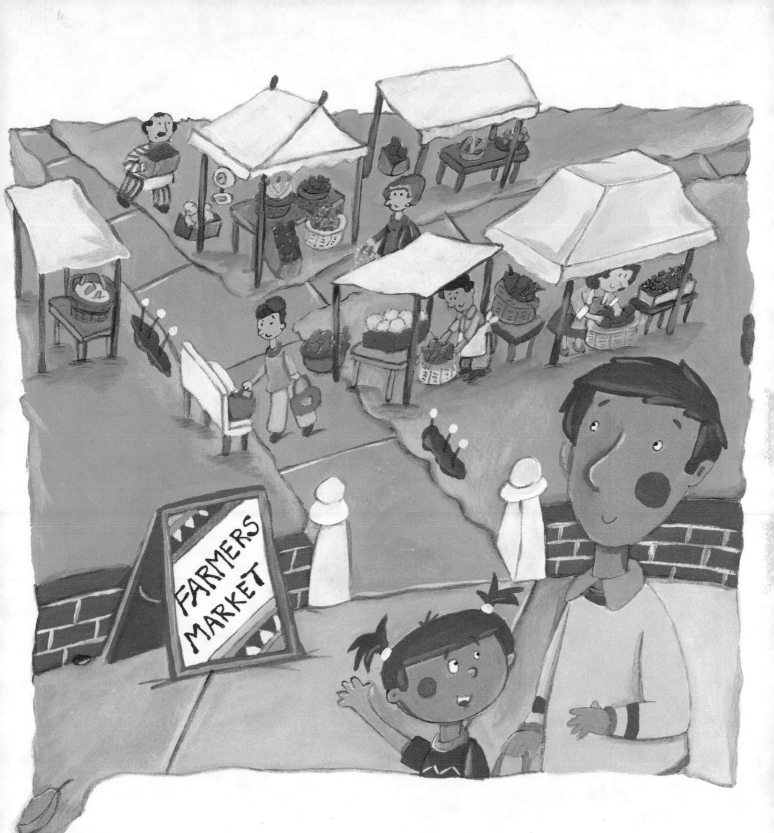

The bus will stop here.

Pam and Dad will have fun.

Look at Viv.

Viv will cut it. It is wet!

Look at Zak.

Zak will sell it.

Dad will get it.

Dad will set it in a bag and zip it.

Look at Bud.

Will you get a yam for me?

Dad and Pam get wet.

They will quit.

Dad and Pam got on the bus.

Dad and Pam had fun.

Envision It! Retell

READING STREET ONLINE
STORY SORT
www.ReadingStreet.com

158

Think Critically

1. A farmers market is a place to buy fruits and vegetables. Name some other places where fruits and vegetables are sold. Text to World

2. Could this story really happen? Explain.

   Realism and Fantasy

3. Look Back and Write Look back at page 155. What can you buy at a farmers market? Write about it.

   TEST PRACTICE | Extended Response

To Market, To Market

To market, to market,
To buy some sweet corn,
Home again, home again,
Blowing a horn!
To market, to market,
To buy tangerines,
Home again, home again,
Eating sardines!

illustrated by Debbie Palen

Objectives
- Understand and use verbs when reading, writing, and speaking.
- Understand and use nouns when reading, writing, and speaking.
- Understand and use adjectives when reading, writing, and speaking.

Let's Write It!

Read Together

Key Features of Sentences with Nouns, Verbs, and Adjectives

- use nouns to tell about people, places, animals, or things

- use verbs to tell about actions

- use adjectives to describe people, places, animals, or things

READING STREET ONLINE
GRAMMAR JAMMER
www.ReadingStreet.com

Expository

Sentences with Nouns, Verbs, and Adjectives

A **sentence** tells a complete idea. A sentence has a verb. Most sentences have a noun. A sentence may have an adjective.

Writing Prompt Think about where you and your family buy food. Write about the place. Use a noun, a verb, and an adjective in your sentence.

Writer's Checklist

Remember, you should . . .

✓ use a noun in your sentence to name a place.

✓ use a verb to tell about an action.

✓ use an adjective to describe something.

The market sells big apples.

The **noun** **market** names the place.

The **verb** **sells** tells about an action.

The **adjective** **big** describes the apples.

Conventions

Sentences

A **sentence** tells a complete idea. It begins with an uppercase letter. Many sentences end with a period. A sentence has a noun and a verb. It can have adjectives to describe. What sentence can you say?

A man likes green beans.

Objectives

• Connect the meaning of a famous story or fable to your own experiences.

Social Studies in Reading

The Maid and the Milk Pail

Read Together

Genre
Fable

- A fable is a short story that teaches a lesson.

- Characters in fables usually learn a lesson from the mistakes they make.

- The author wants readers to connect a fable's lesson to their personal experiences.

- Read "The Maid and the Milk Pail." Think about what you've learned about fables as you read.

A girl took milk to a market. She thought, "I will sell this milk. I will buy a lovely new dress."

162

The girl let go of the pail. It fell. Now the girl could not buy a dress.

Lesson: Don't count on getting something until you actually have it.

Let's **Think** About...

What mistake does the girl make?
Fable

Let's **Think** About...

What lesson does the girl learn? How can you connect this lesson to something that happened to you? **Fable**

Let's **Think** About...

Reading Across Texts When do *Farmers Market* and "The Maid and the Milk Pail" take place? Where do they take place? How do you know?

Writing Across Texts Why are Pam and Dad in *Farmers Market* going to a market? Why is the girl in "The Maid and the Milk Pail" going to a market? Write about their reasons.

Let's Learn It!

Read Together

READING STREET ONLINE
VOCABULARY ACTIVITIES
www.ReadingStreet.com

First, my dad and I went to a farmers market. Then we bought some oranges. Last, we went home and ate them.

Get Ready For Grade 2

Use words such as *first*, *next*, and *last* when you tell a story.

Listening and Speaking

Relate an Experience in Sequence

When we tell about something that happened to us, we use words such as *first*, *then*, *next*, and *last* so that listeners will understand.

Practice It! Think of something that happened to you. Tell others about it. Speak in complete sentences.

Vocabulary

A **noun** is a word that names people, animals, places, or things. We can sort nouns into categories of people, animals, things, and places.

Practice It! Read these words. Identify and sort them into categories of people, animals, things, and places.

dog   **box**   **boy**   **home**

Handwriting

Self-Evaluation During and after writing, make sure your letters are neatly written and formed correctly. Look at the models on pages 174–175. Then write a row of these letters: **Vv   Yy   Zz   Uu   Qq**

Use the models to write these sentences. Leave enough space between the words and sentences.

Val has a quiz.   Val and Quin study.

My Family

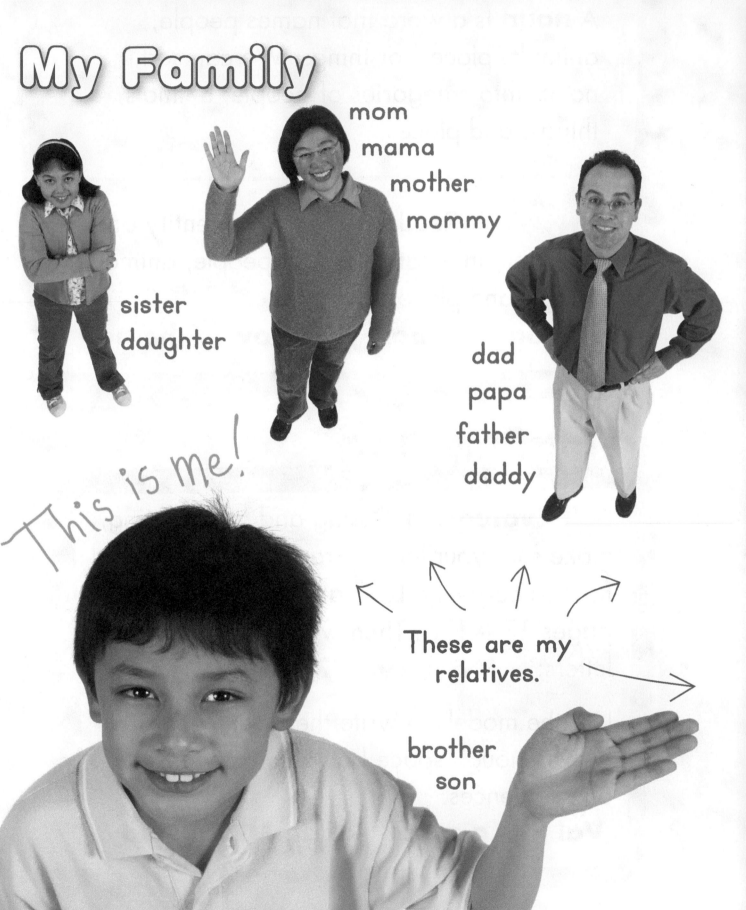

mom
mama
mother
mommy

sister
daughter

dad
papa
father
daddy

This is me!

These are my relatives.

brother
son

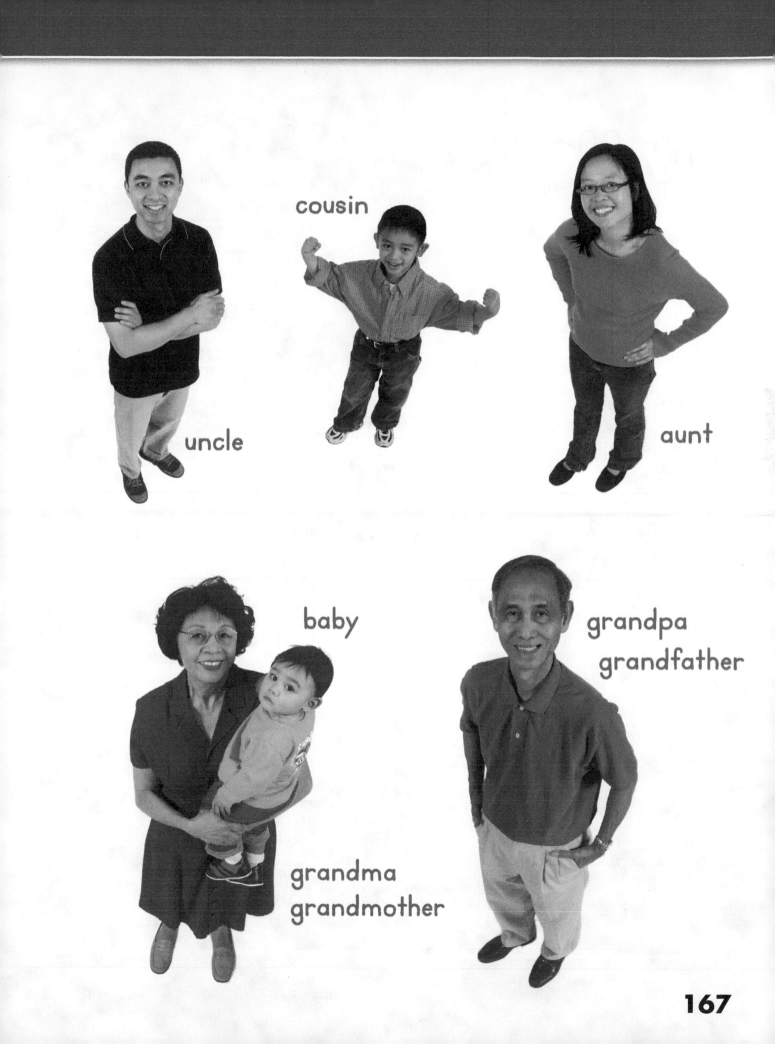

cousin

uncle

aunt

baby

grandpa
grandfather

grandma
grandmother

167

My Home

bookshelf

books

toys

bed

door

window

rug

microwave

stove

refrigerator

sink

counter

desk

chair

couch

carpet

The Market

meat

shopper

cart

groceries

Canne...
Sou...

milk

cheese

banana

grapes

apple

shelves

aisle

lettuce

tomatoes

carrots

Sam

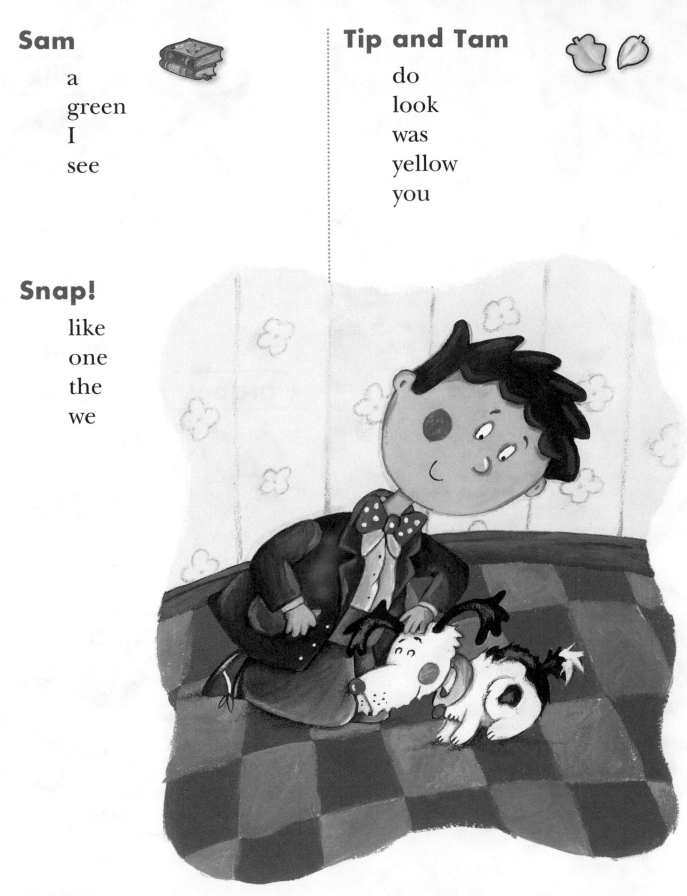

a
green
I
see

Tip and Tam

do
look
was
yellow
you

Snap!

like
one
the
we

The Big Top

are
have
that
they
two

Farmers Market

for
go
here
me
where

School Day

he
is
three
to
with

Aa Bb Cc

Dd Ee Ff

Gg Hh Ii

Jj Kk Ll

Mm Nn Oo

Pp Qq Rr

Ss Tt Uu

Vv Ww Xx

Yy Zz

Acknowledgments

Text

Grateful acknowledgment is made to the following for copyrighted material:

Alfred A. Knopf, Inc., A Division of Random House, Inc. & BookStop Literary Agency, LLC

"School Bus" from *Go! Poetry in Motion* by Dee Lillegard. Copyright © 2006 by Dee Lillegard. Used by permission.

BookStop Literary Agency, LLC

"Bedroom Window" from *Wake Up House! Rooms Full of Poems* by Dee Lillegard. Copyright © 2000 by Dee Lillegard. Used by permission of BookStop Literary Agency, LLC.

Elizabeth M. Hauser

"My Family" from *Rhymes About Us* by Marchette Chute. Copyright © 1974 by E.P. Dutton & Co., Inc.

Note: Every effort has been made to locate the copyright owner of material reproduced on this component. Omissions brought to our attention will be corrected in subsequent editions.

Illustrations

CVR Daniel Moreton

EI2–EI5 Mary Anne Lloyd

EI8–EI17 Chris Lensch

14 Suwin Chan

18 - 27, 45 - 53, 70 - 83, 96 - 122, 125 - 150, 152 - 157 Hector Borlasca

29 Amy Cartwright

32, 33 Nan Brooks

40 Aaron Zenz

55 Wednesday Kirwan

66 Mary Sullivan

94 Miki Sakamoto

95 Lane Gregory

122 Karol Kaminski

150 Stacy Curtis

159 Debbie Palen

162, 163 Luciana Navarro Powell

Photographs

Every effort has been made to secure permission and provide appropriate credit for photographic material. The publisher deeply regrets any omission and pledges to correct errors called to its attention in subsequent editions.

Unless otherwise acknowledged, all photographs are the property of Pearson Education, Inc.

Photo locators denoted as follows: Top (T), Center (C), Bottom (B), Left (L), Right (R), Background (Bkgd)

4 Fuse/Thinkstock; **10** Fuse/Thinkstock; **13** (BR) Monkey Business/Fotolia; **16** (BL) GRIN/NASA; **16** (TCR) Jack Fields/Photo Researchers; **16** (TL) Robert Huberman/Superstock; **16** (BCL) Jupiter Images; **35** (TR) Frank Lukasseck/Getty Images; **35** (TL) Jeremy Woodhouse/Getty Images; **35** (TC) Vrabelpeter1/Fotolia; **36** (Bkgrd) Masterfile Corporation; **40** (BL) Erik Dreyer/Getty Images; **42** Kurhan/Fotolia; **58** Mark Leibowitz/Corbis; **59** (B) JGI/Jamie Grill/Blend Images/Getty Images ; **59** (T) Paul Barton/Corbis; **61** Ellen McKnight/Alamy; **62** (BL) Thinkstock; **62** (Bkgrd) Ariel Skelley/Corbis; **63** Masterfile Corporation; **66** (CL) Rudi Von Briel/PhotoEdit; **66** (TL) Andersen Ross/Photodisc/Getty Images; **68** ©Premaphotos/Nature Picture Library; **84** Stockbyte/Jupiter Images; **85** (T) Bambu Productions/Getty Images; **85** (B) Peter Ravallo/Alamy; **86** John Giustina/Photodisc/Getty Images; **87** (TR) Steffan Hill/Alamy; **88** Jupiter Images; **89** (CR) Blend Images/Getty Images; **89** (BR) Jupiter Images; **94** (TL) Terie Rakke/Getty Images; **94** (CL) Vittorio Bruno/Shutterstock; **111** (T) Mike Clarke/Getty Images; **111** (B) Kim Karpeles/Alamy; **113** Getty Images; **114** Masterfile Corporation; **115** (CR) Masterfile Corporation; **115** (BR) Blend Images/Jupiter Images; **118** (TL) NASA; **118** (CL) AbleStock/Photolibrary/Getty Images; **120** (B) Carleton Chinner/Shutterstock; **136** Anders Ryman/Corbis; **137** (CL) Rafiqur Rahman/Reuters/Corbis; **137** (TC) ©Frans Lemmens/Getty Images; **138** SW Productions/Getty Images; **139** Juniors Bildarchiv/Alamy; **140** (BC) David Grossman/Alamy; **140** (Bkgrd) Heide Benser/zefa/Corbis; **140** (TC) BlueOrange Studio/Fotolia; **144** (BL) Tr3gi/Fotolia; **144** (TL) G. Brad Lewis/Getty Images; **168** (BL) Abode/Beateworks/Corbis; **168** (BR) Arcaid/Alamy; **168** (Bkgrnd) Alamy; **169** (B) Elliott Kaufman/Beateworks/Corbis; **169** (T) Getty Images; **170** (TR) Naka/Fotolia; **170** (Bkgrd) Blue Jean Images/Alamy; **171** (Bkgrd) Getty Images; **171** (BR) D. Hurst/Alamy.

High-Frequency Words

Identify and read the high-frequency words that you have learned. How many words can you read?

Unit R.1
a
green
I
see

Unit R.2
like
one
the
we

Unit R.3
do
look
was
yellow
you

Unit R.4
are
have
that
they
two

Unit R.5
he
is
three
to
with

Unit R.6
for
go
here
me
where

Unit 1.1
come
in
my
on
way

Unit 1.2
she
take
up
what

Unit 1.3
blue
from
get
help
little
use

Unit 1.4
eat
five
four

her
this
too

Unit 1.5
saw
small
tree
your

Unit 1.6
home
into
many
them

Unit 2.1
catch
good
no
put
said
want

Unit 2.2
be
could
horse
of
old
paper

Unit 2.3
live
out
people
who
work

Unit 2.4
down
inside
now
there
together

Unit 2.5
around
find
food
grow
under
water

Unit 2.6
also
family
new
other
some
their

High-Frequency Words

Unit 3.1
always
become
day
everything
nothing
stays
things

Unit 3.2
any
enough
ever
every
own
sure
were

Unit 3.3
away
car
friends
house
our
school
very

Unit 3.4
afraid
again
few
how
read
soon

Unit 3.5
done
know
push
visit
wait

Unit 3.6
before
does
good-bye
oh
right
won't

Unit 4.1
about
enjoy
give
surprise
worry
would

Unit 4.2
colors
draw
drew
great
over
show
sign

Unit 4.3
found
mouth

once
took
wild

Unit 4.4
above
eight
laugh
moon
touch

Unit 4.5
picture
remember
room
stood
thought

Unit 4.6
across
because
dance
only
opened
shoes
told

Unit 5.1
along
behind
eyes
never
pulling
toward

Unit 5.2
door
loved
should
wood

Unit 5.3
among
another
instead
none

Unit 5.4
against
goes
heavy
kinds
today

Unit 5.5
built
early
learn
science
through

Unit 5.6
answered
carry
different
poor

178